BOOKS IN HEBREW
BY MEIR WIESELTIER

*Shirim Itiyim* (Slow poems)
*Makhsan* (Storage)
*Mikhtavim Veshirim Akherim* (Letters and other poems)
*Yi Yevani* (Greek island)
*Qitsur Shnot Hashishim* (The concise sixties)
*Motsa El Hayam* (Exit to the sea)
*Pnim Vakhuts* (Interior and exterior)
*Davar Optimi, Asiyat Shirim* (Something optimistic, the making of poems)
*Kakh* (Take)
*Me'a Shirim* (One hundred poems)
*Perek Alef Perek Bet* (Chapter A chapter B)
*Tiyul B'Iona* (A walk in Iona)

THE FLOWER OF ANARCHY

NATIONAL
ENDOWMENT
FOR THE ARTS

*This project has been supported by an award
from the National Endowment for the Arts.*

**MEIR WIESELTIER**

# THE FLOWER OF ANARCHY

*selected poems*

*Translated from the Hebrew by*
**SHIRLEY KAUFMAN,** *with the author*

*University of California Press*
BERKELEY | LOS ANGELES | LONDON

Cover art for paperback edition: *Window*, by Yaacov Dorchin.
Reproduced by permission.

UNIVERSITY OF CALIFORNIA PRESS
Berkeley and Los Angeles, California

University of California Press, Ltd.
London, England

Library of Congress Cataloging-in-Publication Data
Wieseltier, Meir.
    [Poems. English. Selections]
    The flower of anarchy : selected poems/Meir
  Wieseltier ; translated from the Hebrew
  by Shirley Kaufman, with the author.
      p.      cm.
  ISBN 0-520-23552-5 (cloth : alk. paper)—
  ISBN 0-520-23553-3 (pbk : alk. paper)
    1. Wieseltier, Meir—Translations into English.
I. Kaufman, Shirley. II. Title.
PJ5054.W47 A25 2003
892.4′16—dc21      2002035364
                CIP

Printed in the United States of America
13  12  11  09  08  07  06  05  04  03
10  9  8  7  6  5  4  3  2  1

The paper used in this publication meets the minimum
requirements of ANSI/NISO Z39.48-1992 (R 1997)
(*Permanence of Paper*).

# CONTENTS

FROM *Something Optimistic, the Making of Poems* (1976)

FROM *Exit to the Sea* (1981)

FROM *Letters and Other Poems* (1986)

FROM *Storage* (1995)

## FROM *Slow Poems* (2000)

## ACKNOWLEDGMENTS

Many of these translations were published in earlier versions in the following journals:

*American Poetry Review:* "The Secret of Authority," "Wives of October" (25, no. 6, Nov./Dec. 1996); "Abraham," "Sealed in a Bottle," "Pro & Con" (Nov./Dec. 2002).

*Field:* "The Fowl of the Air," "Thin Livestock," "Window to the Future" (no. 53, fall 1995).

*The Jerusalem Quarterly:* "Every arm," "Remembering" (no. 4, summer 1977).

*The Kenyon Review:* "Letter 2," "Letter 3" (15, no. 4, fall 1993).

*Leviathan Quarterly* (England): "Passengers" (no. 5, Sept. 2002); "On Wonders" (no.6, Dec. 2002).

*The Literary Review:* "A dull khaki light comes down again" (26, no. 2, winter 1983).

*Lyric Poetry Review:* "The World Is Full of the Righteous" and "Words for Music" (no. 4 summer/fall 2003).

*Modern Poetry in Translation* (London): "Isaac's Story," "Soliloquy of Dada the Cat," "Cheese," "The Head" (no. 14, winter 1998–99).

*The Nation:* "Sonnet: Against Making Blood Speak Out" (April 15, 2002).

*Southern Humanities Review:* "Burning Holy Books" (30, no. 1, winter 1996).

*Translation* (Columbia University): "Letter 1," "Output" (28, spring 1993).

*TriQuarterly:* "Friends," "A Request," "March" (no. 39, spring 1977).

"*In Camera*" and "Fruit" appeared first in *New Writing in Israel*, edited by Ezra Spicehandler, Schocken Books, 1976.

"A Dream of Death as an Angel" appeared first in *New Writing from Israel*, edited by Jacob Sonntag, Corgi Books, London, 1976 and also in *The Burning Bush*, edited by Moshe Dor and Natan Zach, W.H. Allen, London, 1977.

I would like to acknowledge Gabriel Levin for his earlier translations of some of these poems, which provided me with a way into the work. I cherish the friendship and help of Shlomith Rimmon-Kenan, who led me through my very first translations of Wieseltier and other Hebrew poets. I am grateful to Shimon Sandbank for his suggestions, and to Peter Cole, who first made me think this book was possible and whose notes and comments on the entire manuscript were insightful and of great value. Chana Kronfeld also encouraged this project from the beginning, and her generosity of spirit and knowledge of the Hebrew language—with all its history, wordplay, and staggering challenge—her attention to every nuance of tone and meaning, line by line, were of immeasurable help and inspiration to me. I also appreciate Chana Bloch's comments on the poetry in English, and the discerning efficiency of Mia Barzilai, who prepared the final manuscript for publication.

To my husband, Bill Daleski, my loving thanks for his wisdom and critical skill, his sensitivity to the English language, and his patient reading of the Hebrew with the English over the many years I've worked on these translations.

The unstinting cooperation of the poet himself, Meir Wieseltier, throughout the years of decisions and indecisions, is acknowledged more fully in "Working with the Poet: A Translator's Response."

S.K.

In a world where managing the news is more urgent than trying to understand the history behind it, or the forces that shape it, comes Meir Wieseltier, all six feet, three inches of him, with his halo of silvery white hair, looking like an aging basketball player or an unbearded, misplaced prophet walking his English setter through the traffic-snarled streets of south Tel-Aviv, releasing his torrent of words for many Israelis unable to cope, punching holes in what's left of our frayed representations of love and war.

> I can't stand political poetry: that civil and prophetic posturing
> (Why should anyone speak in broken lines?)

These lines from "Pro & Con," which was published in 1983, call on the poet to be silent:

> let the poet turn inward, let him study his navel,
> dream of his father and mother,
> or draw pigeons on the neighbor's roof
> a street in the city, a house on the street,
> a room inside the house, an orange peel on the table
> slowly
> drying

But he goes on to say

> sometimes I can't control myself, and like a pervert
> I sneak up on the wax figures' display.
> Here they are lined up in a row, these gawky masks in charge
> of deciding our fate

The sight of these leaders posing "with the postures of men who get things done. . . smiling their smiles almost like humans" drives him, in the end, in a furious closing stanza, to incoherence.

. . .

Meir Wieseltier first brought me some of his poems to translate for the Spring 1977 issue of the Chicago journal *TriQuarterly*, which featured contemporary Israeli literature. It was soon after I arrived in Israel. Our friendship started in a cloud of smoke from his Gauloises cigarettes (which I managed to survive) and grew over the many years that followed. As we consulted, argued, and read his poems together, I refined my understanding and struggled to transform his Hebrew words—their sense and sound—into English (American, really) poems.

Wieseltier, who rails against "political poetry" in the poem quoted above, has written the most powerful poems of social and political protest in Israel, poems that are tragically timeless, like "Sonnet: Against Making Blood Speak Out," published in 1984:

If I die one day from the bullet of a young killer
. . . or in a bomb explosion while I'm checking the price
of cucumbers in the market, don't dare say
that my blood permits you to justify your wrongs.

A deeply caring part of him, along with his critical awareness, temper his fury. He is no longer the "bad boy" of the sixties (there were some would-be Allen Ginsbergs and dadaists in those days enlivening Tel-Aviv in smoke-filled cafes and in new little magazines, some of which Wieseltier edited), when he and a few other young poets, especially Yonah Wallach and Ya'ir Hurwitz, were exposing every human and inhuman frailty, turning traditional Hebrew poetry inside out, making the ancient Hebrew language new for their generation, as Yehuda Amichai, the most accomplished and admired poet of the preceding generation, and Natan Zach had done in their time.

Now Wieseltier, in an age of cyberspace and terrorism and damaged hope, is the distinguished recipient of the Israel Prize, his country's highest honor, awarded on Independence Day in the millennial year 2000 in the presence of the Israeli establishment (president, prime minister, minister of education, chief justice of the Supreme Court, mayor of Jerusalem, and so on) to its most antiestablishment poet. A poet of intense engagement, historical awareness, and verbal power, he was given "the highest possible honor in Israel for his long-standing, subversive work," according to one critic at the time.

But there is more to Wieseltier than subversion. The accumulation of tragicomic detail in his poems, black humor, and visceral imagery offers no escape from the-way-it-is. His words force us to confront the absurd and seamy side of life, head-on. One of his most stunning early poems, "Isaac's Story," is about child abuse in a shabby Tel-Aviv office and was written in the early seventies, before the avalanche of such stories and poems. The sexually charged language focuses on the surroundings and pathos of the boy, who finally found a summer job when he was picked up in the steaming streets of the first modern city on the Mediterranean coast.

. . .

Wieseltier has been strongly rooted in Tel-Aviv, ever since he came to live and go to school there in 1955, cherishing his love-hate relationship with the city, poking into its darkest corners with cool appraisal, even its unbuilt subway ("Weather," "Isaac's Story," "Skywriting," "Naive Painting," "The Man at the Piano," "The Tel-Aviv Subway"). He is equally at home in the Hebrew Bible, often using its ancient phrases as well as its characters to illuminate contemporary disasters. All his distrust of the rhetoric of religious devotion culminates in the last couplet of the final stanza of "Abraham":

Abraham didn't value a thing in the world but God.
Against Him, he never sinned, no difference between them.

Unlike Isaac who loved his uncouth son, unlike Jacob
who slaved for women, who limped from God's thrashing all night,
who saw angeled ladders only in dreams. Not Abraham.
He loved God and God loved him. And together
they counted the righteous in the cities before wiping them out.

. . .

In making a representative selection from more than forty years of
Wieseltier's poems, I discovered that my decisions about which poems to
translate had been highlighting continuing themes: they were anticlerical
("A Request," "Adoshem," "Burning Holy Books"), antigovernment ("The
Secret of Authority," "Garbage Dump 2000," "Pro & Con"), antiwar, and
antimilitary ("Song of the Last Soldier," "Call-Up," "Salt on the Wounds
of the Land," "To Be Continued"). Some of Wieseltier's work is even anti-
poetry, demonstrating his profound skepticism of poetry as communica-
tion in poems such as "Take" and "Poetry Swallowed."

Wieseltier can be merciless in his polemic against state-funded ortho-
dox religious coercion or political rot and wrongheadedness, but slyly
comic at the same time. From the beginning of his career, he has converted
despair and disgust into wit and irony, with hard-hitting language and a
wry smile. His voice is alternately anarchic and involved, angry and caring,
serious and hilarious, cacophonous and lyric. "The Soliloquy of Dada the
Cat" is an exquisite rendering of that voice. Here are the first few lines:

I was scrawny as a wormy branch
going wild in trash cans, and I was a pampered pet
stuffed with prime turkey to restore me, and then again
I was a beloved kitty fattened with a baby bottle,
and I was a neglected cat, kicked down the stairs or out into the
     yard,
revived.

. . .

There is more pain than bitterness in many of Wieseltier's recent poems, as in his anguish over the disastrous midair collision of two Israeli helicopters filled with seventy-three young Israeli soldiers on their way to the war in Lebanon ("On the Seventy-three"). Pain overrides rage in lines like these:

> all these corpses and wounded and disabled are so real
> that any rhetoric is beyond them, their lives are finished
> their likely screams have faded somewhere in Lebanon.

Still, there is a strongly affirmative resonance beyond the sorrows and futilities in many of these poems, an enduring resonance, as in "The Flower of Anarchy," a love poem from which the title of this book is taken. Freedom, the essential spirit of anarchy, waves its banners, and even its dog's ears ("Poems with a Dog, 3"), throughout Wieseltier's work, as does freedom from State, from religion, from any apparatus or relationship that would constrict or shackle it. But apart from Bakunin, and earlier writers and philosophers, Wieseltier seems closest to the American poet Hayden Carruth, an anarchist by his own definition: "no doctrine, no ideology . . . no party line, no required procedure, no orthodoxy." These have been Wieseltier's guiding principles throughout his writing career. As Dada the cat says in the last line of his soliloquy, like God to Moses (and like Popeye too): "I am what I am."

Love is a well-explored theme here—love of memorable women, and for his mother, in the compassionate "Letter 1" and "Letter 2." His work is full of zest for experience, notably in his travels, and a voracious appetite for life. He displays a lonely yet comic sense of himself as a defender of human values ("I Ask Myself") and human foolishness ("Musée Picasso"). He enjoys the influence of many poets in other languages: Apollinaire, Mallarmé, Neruda, Cavafy, Yeats, Eliot, Cummings, Pound. It is not easy to balance all this with the rage against everything wrong in our place and in our time. But has it ever been different for poetry?

.   .   .

Meir Wieseltier was born in Moscow in 1941 and taken in the same year by his mother with two older sisters on a half-starving trek to Novosibirsk in southwestern Siberia, when hundreds of thousands of people—women, children, and the aged—were evacuated from Moscow because of the war. He never knew his father, who was killed as a soldier in the Soviet Army in Leningrad. After the war and the wandering with his family as a DP through Poland, Germany, and France, he arrived in Israel in 1949, the first year of the newly declared State. A bittersweet nostalgia for his preteen years, uncorrupted by symbols of nationalistic fervor, in the small town of Netanya, is lyrically caught in "Far from the Flag Parade," included in his latest book:

> It was sweet, dark, and tangy
> under the heavy branches
> of the citrus trees bent
> around Ein-Hatkehelt and Avikhail.
> I called it homeland.
> Shade streaming from the trees,
> the heavy heads of the Shamutti oranges
> scattered around me,
> a glowing, saturated yours-for-the-taking,
> far from the flag parade,
> I called it homeland.
> That was a long time ago. A kind of piratical act
> of a boy who found
> something he wasn't looking for.

. . .

This is the first book-length collection of Meir Wieseltier's poetry in English. In Hebrew he is a master of word games, extended metaphor, alliteration, onomatopoeia, and rhyme, often juxtaposing biblical archaic Hebrew with the colloquial. Every translator of Hebrew poetry faces the impossible task of transferring the freshness, the emotional precision, the poetic skill, the layering of meaning in the Hebrew words and the three root letters that make up the words, into another language—into poetry, with the original passion and meaning. The music.

I have been especially fortunate to work with the poet himself in the making of this book, and to listen to his voice. I am grateful for his poems, and for his invaluable help in bringing them into English.

Shirley Kaufman

Jerusalem, 2003

# EARLY POEMS (1960–1969)

## KINGCHILD

There's a small child sitting on an egg,
for many years he has loved a dead king.
The song of the egg sounds to him
like the king's speech in a stately hall.
He can't tell that his own song is climbing,
eating at treetops until tattered
leaves fall down his neck
and his hair turns white as an echo.

The child becomes king,
the king is buried beneath a stone,
a bird won't know a thing
between hatching and dying.
Warm blood soaks the eyes of dew,
a glimmer comes, then it goes.
There's a king sitting on an egg.
There's a child buried beneath a stone.

My favorite weather in the whole world
is Tel-Aviv weather on a winter night.
Tel-Aviv, like a woman shoved with her clothes on
into a bathtub. Thugs did this to her, and now she staggers
shamed through the streets, begging for mercy.

Show some mercy to this city, say something kind to her.

Air dampened the sand and refreshed it. Now this sweet humidity
wanders half-awake, delighted, the whole night before it.
Strokes her cheek as it passes, but won't pause.
Trills of moisture slip between cubes of houses,
peeling the plaster. Tel-Aviv falls asleep
on her feet, and moans in her slumber.

Say something kind, she deserves a little pity.

My heart was composed of makeup, its secrets
dissolving, half-revealed to me alone,
mixed with and next to my life,
there were birds nesting in me.
Dangerous beasts paced through me as if down a hall.
Whispers, conjured from inside, hid
my mysteries from me. I depended
on wonders. On what else if not
for such splendor. I'd crouch over myself
as if over the mouth of a well, the secret
of my grim childhood always dangling from my neck.
Wherever I went my arrival was known,
and someone who'd waited for years
would fall all over me. I was embarrassed.
I tolled like a bell. I had dinosaur bones
that creaked and sang.

## BALLAD

I killed a fly with Cummings' poems;
it was morning, early morning,
my groin still throbbed from you
(but my heart and eyes were aching),
and gingerly holding the book,
I crushed a fly with Cummings' poems.

The fly preferred flesh to plaster,
the ceiling all white again without the imperious black spot
now on my nose, and it entered the pages of the book,
as though it had never heard of the architectural mania of Minos,
and it was very early in the morning,
I crushed a fly with Cummings' poems.

When I reopen the book after getting some sleep,
after breakfast at midday,
the fly will fall out and no longer be relevant,
but somehow it's hard to explain how
I killed a fly with Cummings' poems.

## DADDY AND MOMMY WENT TO THE MOVIES, ILANA STAYS ALONE IN THE ARMCHAIR LOOKING AT A GRAY BOOK

She turns the pages, naked uncles
so naked and skinny, run and
even aunties with fannies showing
and others in pajamas as in a show
with yellow cloth stars sewed on.
And everybody so ugly and thin,
and big round eyes like chickens.

It's awfully weird, so gray. Ilana has pencils—red
and blue and green and yellow and pink.
So she goes to her room
and takes all the beautiful pencils
and draws with great flair
glasses and funny faces on all of them.
Especially on that bald skinny boy,
she gives him a big red mustache
and perched at the tip of the mustache—a bird.

I saw three baby-faced Germans
sitting in Café Notre Dame.
They were so soft in the morning
those three baby-faced Germans,
their field-grass hair
and their barefoot faces.

It rained on the city and the Seine,
washing trash into the gutter,
stale spit and yesterday's headlines,
hitting the Notre Dame and the Seine
and dripping on the eyelashes of passers-by
who moved in an endless line as if weeping
past windows that creaked on their hinges
in front of three baby-faced Germans.

The world is full of the righteous—
all of us are righteous in our own eyes
drink from our own cups, sit on our own butts
have some pangs of conscience, find our way out
arrange times for meditation, times for tears
lock ourselves in with a little key
and pocket it,
then sleep: and nurture
the shards of our anger.

## ABRAHAM

The only thing in the world Abraham loved was God.
He didn't love the gods of others. Those people
slept with their wives every night and stuffed themselves with meat and
     wine.
Their gods were made of wood or clay and painted vermilion,
then sold like onions in the market to the highest bidder.
He figured out his own God, and made himself His chosen.

He loved that God above everything else in the world.
He wouldn't bow to the gods of others; he told them: if you go right
I'll go left, if you go left, I'll go right.
He told them: you can't accuse me of a get-rich scheme.
He refused to give or take anything
except with God. If only He'd asked
He'd have got it. Anything. Even Isaac the only son, the trusting heir
(but if there's a God, there's an angel).

Abraham didn't value a thing in the world but God.
Against Him, he never sinned, there was no difference between them.
Unlike Isaac who loved his uncouth son, unlike Jacob
who slaved for women, who limped from God's thrashing all night,
who saw angeled ladders only in dreams.
Not Abraham. He loved God and God loved him.
And together they counted the righteous of the cities before wiping
     them out.

## TAKE A LOOK AT MY REBELS

*Verses on a theme of Jerusalem and feet,
wood, and fire*

Take a look at my rebels
my spindly-legged rebels,
Yokhanan of Gush-Halav was scrawny and beloved
and Shimon of the Desert
had flat feet.
(Not one cross on Golgotha
                              but three
and in Galilee they cried over twice as many.)
The one who hammered the nails was a master craftsman
and the one who prepared the crosses worked with honest hands.
The WPA in the Roman workshop
                              drudged
in the streets of Jerusalem.

Where housing projects stand now, crosses once dreamed
of more newcomers.
Rain fell like a grid, and blood
soaked into the dust and the wood.
Hearts churned with vengeance
red and clenched.
And my rebels drank cheap wine and said:
We'll drink a toast yet in Pilate's cellar.
Under their robes they were spindly and wasted
and their feet were flat.

Yokhanan of Gush-Halav was scrawny and beloved
and had never seen Bar Giora.
(In Galilee the sign of a cross against the sky
was no big deal.)

Josephus didn't tell you any of this
                              but he knew
they would not drink a toast in Pilate's cellar
(Pilate was already dead)
and his heart was as cold
as a Roman legion
against the alleys of Jerusalem.

        .   .   .

My rebels were dressed
like wind-ravaged trees.
They knew they'd only find peace
at the end on a bed of fire.

Bar Giora tarried in the desert
and the ones in Jerusalem wanted to rest and buy protection
while in Gush-Halav people played
with iron
and prepared for surgical intervention.

Rain stuttered on the roofs
                              and sputtered
tunes.
Covered in heavy hoods, drowsy-eyed
lizard legions rolled through the mud.
At dawn blue penciled
crosses appeared against the sky.

And when a new governor was appointed,
he shook hands with all the centurions
and the elders of Jerusalem.
The city swayed as on a swing.
My rebels stared
drank cheap wine and spoke:

but sometimes the words stuck on their lips
and they pressed against the window, and heard the thump
of hammers in honest hands.

## SONG OF THE LAST SOLDIER

A song of the last soldier
in a regiment that wasn't wiped out until
one day it turned out to be expendable.
And a flag as good as orphaned
was placed in the blackening forest,
and anyone not shooting himself
hung on in that blackness until he vanished,
winds wailed through his ribs
and settled down in his skull.

But I packed a knapsack
of brass insignia, turning black
as the trees.
That same day
I ate roots and mushrooms,
fell asleep on a branch
without dreaming.

Yesterday, and the day before
the sky didn't preach peace,
didn't preach anything.
What was done was allowed,
the rain came down unblinking.
I saw my unblinking brothers
change into wood.

I saw the wind's laughter
and a faithless earth sprout with buds.

I'm going back.
This morning I'll walk
through familiar land, earth trampled
by frenzied marches.
I don't care if mushrooms
are in the way. I'll sit down
at noon and eat. When I've finished
I won't bury the scraps.
In the late afternoon a red sun
will spread its fire and show me
no matter how hard I look
for the track I know, no matter how far I go
I still won't reach the main path
that gets me out of the forest,
into a past that once had a future.

I saw the wind's laughter
and a faithless earth sprout with buds.
I'm going back. This morning I'll walk
through familiar land.

Every poet thinks sometimes
he's the last poet in the world.
How else could it be?
The world's all dust and consuming flames,
every grocery a volcano.
The world is muddy ripples
and smashing rocks,
and Poetry?
Poetry's swallowed up. Illegitimate daughter
of man's plots against Nature,
of the lust to couple and grab.

Someone is singing, might sing again,
can't hear you, won't hear you:
too much noise
that's more urgent, louder, lasting.
Poetry's swallowed up.
      (It's like an unnamed island
      in the misnamed Pacific Ocean:
      some captain reported
      he'd seen it. A geological mission
      had already found it flooded. Some
      hopefuls with exaggerated earnestness
      sailed out to explore it, and
      hit a sand bank)

# THE FAMOUS PEPPERS OF MRS. ALMOZLINO

Death caught Mrs. Almozlino by the throat.
It wasn't nice of him,
it was rude.
Mrs. Almozlino writhed in the clutches of that psychopath.
The stuffed peppers sizzled on the flame,
a delicious smell filled the whole kitchen.
Mr. Applestein smelled it on the staircase and envied Mr. Almozlino.
Mr. Almozlino glanced at his watch and smiled to himself.
Ruth Almozlino, married to Yoram Shaked, parked her car.
Mrs. Almozlino tried to grab hold of the table but didn't make it.
Shaul Almozlino came out of the officers' mess speaking to Sergeant
    Drora as they walked.

Mrs. Almozlino shed all her shame.
Mrs. Almozlino toppled like a bottle.
The next day Mr. Applestein told Mrs. Cohen: we're lucky the whole
    house didn't catch fire.

## SOMETIMES MACBETH

Sometimes Macbeth sits on the terrace.
Sun strokes the palms of his hands.
He's dreaming of flowers for the birthday
of his crazy Lady.

He looks with indifference
at the royal graveyard.
In the sun it's like any other garden.
White swans floating on the lake.

Steam slides down the kitchen windows.
Fat horses chomp their straw in the stables.
Someone comes in at the gate, locks it behind him.
He has a word with the gardener, who shows him a new variety of rose.

Everything's clear as far as Birnam, hills swathed in green.
A sweet sleep presses his eyelids down.

## THE JOURNEY OF THE GREAT EGYPTIAN OBELISK
## TO THE WEST

*After the gilded inscription on its base
at Place de la Concorde, Paris*

*What an obelisk looks like*
Long, hard, and pointed.
That's what the gods have made for us,
that's why we've been making gods
for six thousand years.

*In higher echelons*
A tyrant's life is hard,
says one tyrant to another.
Life's hard anyway,
it pays to adore
it pays to be adored.

*Seamen's observations*
The great Mediterranean is no match
for the latest technical innovations
of 1866;
the obelisk *magnifique*
navigates like the Golden Fleece.

*Remark of the French historian*
Where once foundations were laid
for civilizations and manners,
now the primitive fellah
dwells with his ass and goat
in a clay hut.

We in the West
engraved on every coin
Equality Liberty Fraternity.
Napoleon after Napoleon
marches ahead of us now.

*Conversation of a French foreman*
Three and a half damn months
in the stinking orient and on the Mediterranean
just to move this slab of an obelisk
from place to place.
In the meantime Jean-Paul has slept with Claudette
and Jean-Baptiste is not my son:
but I'm better off than Jean-Pierre
who's buried near a German village.
Now they are putting up that stone
on a stone in the heart of the square.
*Bon dieu,* if they were smart
they would surround it with a *pissoir.*

*German tourist's letter*
Have you managed to see the obelisk
they erected on the Place de la Concorde?
Stuck up like the noses of the French,
a people of wine-swilling frogs.

Berlin would have been better,
on top of the Chancellor's helmet.

*An Egyptian porter has the last word*
There came those effendis of Nabulioon
and dragged a stone into the sea.
The Faranji are all crazy.
Allah have pity on the believers.
I got two dinars.

## I ASK MYSELF

Do I
   really
      want
         a job
            policing
the imagination
in a police force stationed on rooftops
hanging around doorways, staircases
glancing at my watch, swinging a club, easily controlling
   demonstrations
orderly in the end, with a permit from the municipality:
you've got a permit, you've got order
and that's it.
The main thing is the finish line
where I patrol, should I patrol, a top-sergeant you don't fool around
   with,
keeping a sure watch on all the forces assembled from everywhere
deployed in the side alleys, on the doorsteps
ready for action in case there's a clash,
if there's a clash, if something spills
in the wrong channel, according to
permits never issued—

Should I, stupid helmet on my head, tin shield
in left hand, whistle in mouth,
club ready in right hand,

feeling the nervous air,
advance like a ladybug into Purim carnivals
to drum on painted boards, papier-mâché, ankles in confetti
smashing unruly limbs in hunger strikes brandishing bread signs
directing political protests back to the buses
advising everyone to go home
bobbing here and there through bunches of hooting boys
in the gridlocked arteries of vital roads—

Should I at last make a contented survey
of streets almost entirely emptied
as the first evening lights come on, a small
wind swoops over my shoulder, lifting
a huge pile of paper trash, torn cardboard, shreds of slogans, orange
    peel, empty cigarette cartons, one baby sock

from nowhere in crazy
slow motion, heart twisting
across streets disappearing in the dying light
into the sewers—

Should I finally sit down in my pajamas opposite the fridge
drinking sweet coffee chewing an avocado sandwich
after a workday that's brought order into a world
of disorder, stopped floods before they could wipe out
people, houses, a whole city, wondering

who else would have done it
imagining how bad
things might have been without me
and what a grand dedicated operation
it takes to maintain a civilization—.

Take poems but don't read them,
do violence to this book:
spit on it, kick it,
wring its neck.

Throw this book in the sea
to see if it can swim.
Hold it over a gas stove
to see if it doesn't burn.
Nail it, saw through it
to see if it resists.

This book is a paper rag,
letters like flies—and you
are a rag of flesh: you eat dust, ooze
blood, stare at it, and snooze.

## FRIENDS

Friends come and talk, they talk and you talk
and eight, ten, fourteen
eyes hover fidgety, desperate, gnats
in their search for honey, jam,
anything sweet, anything sticky for the soul.

They sit they get up they drink with long-practiced hope.
And the soul, juice drained out, begs to be sweet.
Somebody gives you a look as if passing a note:

and you put the note in your pocket, with a glance that opens a door.
And he nods that it's OK to talk, you don't need notes anymore.

## A REQUEST

The day I die or the day after
I'd like some friends to come down,
take a day off from work
and gather around what's left of me.

And not be ashamed of how few they are,
and firmly, even with sticks if they have to,
shoo from my corpse those black crows
that drag dead bodies to their graves.

Let them lift me and seat me in the car,
without covering my face, without ritual cleansing,
and go with me as far as we have to go
to a wooded place on the Carmel or in Galilee.

And dig a hole wide enough and deep
and not hurry to drop me in, but sit down and smoke
a cigarette over my flesh and features
whose nonexistence is imminent.

As long as they don't sit with heads sunk and silent,
but talk together like human beings,
not separate beings, creatures alone,
but seeping through each other, people like sieves.

And finally they'll have to lower the body—
the day goes down, the body's let down—and shovel in the soil
and stack up the stones against wild animals
and soil on the stones for the grass to cover again.

And from then on, to keep the place secret,
so audacious authorities can't
turn the whole thing upside down
and pluck the corpse out of the ground.

This job has to be done, so let it be done by friends
who won't strip the body of its soaking clothes,
or wrap it in white cloth like a mummy,
or mumble the fraudulent mumble of dealers in death.

And though I urge my friends in the clearest terms
so they can withstand a criminal charge,
I'm afraid they'll go soft and not do what I ask,
and some will give thanks if they don't,

and walk half-hearted behind the cart
which pious crooks rattle in the limestone road,
and in spite of themselves, listen to the foul blessings,
and perform the farce of rending their clothes, then toss the first earth.

So don't be put off if I seem obsessed
with the style of my burial, or ask for something special.
As long as there's love, there has to be burial.
I only wanted you to know how things stand.

. . . and I'll also remember you like a black balloon
in a cloud greenish-gray
between Dover and Calais
in a fierce wind
on the first, exactly the first
of January, '70.

And like a flock of trained parachutists,
the days of the year had already been set
to jump in the gut of the plane's silhouette
that droned in the distance,

but your own gaze clung
to a whiteness of gulls that hung

above our heads; you saw only
a flock of birds frozen in flight

and me like a white balloon
that carried you along

and would carry you wherever it went
on the wings of a seasoned wind,

and from the porthole the cooks
applaud you and salute

you and your belly
full of flowers.

And only the ferry, I suppose
comes close tonight as it did on that evening
to the feet of the cliffs melting
in the moist dark.

## ISAAC'S STORY

A violent story about the boy call him Isaac one day
Isaac went looking for work since it was the summer break
and Isaac was supposed to find work and work was found for him in a
    spinning mill
where Tel-Aviv runs into Jaffa between a seventeen-year-old worker
    who fastened an old smock over her breasts and panties
and a mouse in the shape of a man named Eliahu who would push his
    hand between the two halves of her buttocks
every chance he had and the loom is a hellish instrument that doubles
    the time and triples and septuples it to destroy you
the loom's caught in your mouth between your teeth and you're
    between its teeth and between the teeth of mouse Eliahu and
    between her panties which show from time
to time floating on a sea of desire churned in a haze
—terrible especially after the noon break dragged back to the loom in a
    rasping tin halter
Isaac stands in a damp undershirt longing to be a thread oh a thread in
    her panties
and Mister Levkovitz in ex-British mandate khakis complete with
    kneesocks complete with a sort of khaki safari hat with air vents like
    some goddamn explorer in Africa
comes by and digs his finger into the damp undershirt and hot flesh to
    the core of his belly
and asks how it goes with my servant Jacob may dogs lick up your
    blood and harlots wash themselves in it
and here's the true story of Isaac's flight through summer dust and
    chariots of soot on Salameh Road

in his checked shirt stuck to his undershirt stuck to the skin to the
   flesh to the bone to the marrow
on foot to Moshavot Square where Zionism is laid out at the crossroad
   like an open book and Egged buses ride over it
and via Petach Tikva Road to the Maariv newspaper building where the
   smell of the air-conditioning streams out of the entrance like the
   smell of a lie from the mouth of a liar
heading for the junction of Petach Tikva and Hamasger Roads and
   Hasmonean Street
where a motorcycle goes off the road and brakes and rattles next to him
   its rider a weasel-faced man
with sunglasses and a drooping cap and soggy shirt and a pair of shorts
   bulging over his belly
and the arms and legs naked something thick and heavy and flaccid and
   twisted and damp
and the weasel face asks Isaac in a hot drawl where he's going
and Isaac answers he's looking for a summer job
and the weasel face points to the back seat of the motorcycle that will
   take him to a job because he has a driving school and an office
and Isaac on the motorcycle that stirs summer wind out of nothing and
   rattles south to Lilienblum Street across from the old Eden movie
   theater
and the man leads him into a yard full of dust and stones and rusty
   pickle cans children are playing with
and through a piss-soaked back entrance Isaac follows a pair of legs
   that seem boneless to the top of a flight of stairs
up to a toiletlike door with a sign DRIVING SCHOOL and in the room

as wide as the big window with its filthy curtain and about twice as
   long
a table with two drawers and one chair and a framed license to run a
   driving school for motorcycles and an unmade bed
and over the bed in a gilt frame the heavily bearded, sober face of a
   Sephardi rabbi and his wife in her headband and earrings
unbelievably the parents of the weasel-faced man
staring in faded sepia forever and the room too narrow for their gaze
and the weasel face takes a stack of Ministry of Transport virgin forms
   out of the drawer and a faded notebook and stamps with an ink pad
and he tells Isaac to sit on the chair next to the table and fill out every
   form with names and details from the notebook
and sign them with the stamp at the bottom
and that's the whole job Isaac is uneasy I have lots of work for you
   promises the weasel face
and Isaac with perfect penmanship page after virgin page makes entries
   in green ink with a stamp at the end
what's easier thinks Isaac now taking it easy in the room's coolness
when the hand that has dropped as if by accident on his knee slides
   over the smoothness of his thigh and into the fly of his shorts
a steamy damp hand touches him there and a hot breath in his ear
   whispers don't be afraid
and Isaac not taking flight just then and something sticks to his neck
   and says it'll be worth your while I'll pay you lots
and Isaac doesn't move and a hand grabs the curve of his buttock and a
   voice says sweetie I'll give you great pleasure

and Isaac's straining eyes cling to the heavily bearded Sephardi rabbi
  and his wife with her earrings and headband
and Isaac's young hard-on like a young gazelle in the room
leaping because he's already without pants and the snout of the weasel
  sucking so piously at his feet
and a short time after in the street and in his pocket ten liras and in his
  underpants like a wet kitten

## CALL-UP

So they'll call the Little Prince
stick a submachine gun in his hand and say:
you might have come from another star
but now you're here
and that's not an elephant you see
from under the painted hat, but a tank.
The lamplighter's a terrorist,
and if you don't wipe out those sheep
it'll be your head instead.
That's how it is, little prince.

At the end of Independence Day 1972
a small plane goes up
in the Tel-Aviv evening sky,
a line of skywriting
trails out of its belly:
  *No work in your kitchen with Deli Chicken!*

In a little café
on Dizengoff between Nordau Boulevard
and the police headquarters of the Northern Precinct
still lit up by a seven-branched menorah and rows
of light bulbs,
a small circle sits
watching TV
and between one song and another
they drink a last cup of coffee
before going to bed.

Not a sound in the neighborhood,
last night's circus is over,
everything returns to its place as fast as expected:
customers to the café, children home,

flags to the closet, angst to the heart,
the two regular whores to Levinsky's doorway
and the alarm to six o'clock.

On darkening balconies
a man and a woman, fiftyish, stand
in their pajamas assessing the evening.
They are one meter apart.
They don't speak
or look at each other
as if there's no common
language in this land.

Oh, Tel-Aviv the Great,
city in the dark, would-be celebration,
strange holiday of stammering jabber
oh TV
oh buses
oh taxis
oh Jews.

## Adoshem

I know these people,
I know what they're up to,
I've listened to their souls breathing
in the cold and in their adversity
and on the day of their heart's joy,
praying to the God of the Jews.

I know this spectacle,
I've stood there watching them
load the lame God of the Jews on their backs
and set forth with him in a caravan
to march down the roads of the world
with their staffs and their bundles.

Whoever has not seen the God of the Jews exiled in their midst
has never set eyes on God's face.

Not on Mount Sinai nor in Solomon's temple
but cast out in the world,
carried on the backs of these people
like some half-baked matzo,
the God of the Jews became a god
the likes of which had never been seen.

And he will reign over them,
a toothless god,
face of an old hag and brittle bones—
from generation to generation. He will reign forever.

The world is a tiny star,
a bulb of forty watts,
airplanes come like moths
streaking from side to side.

The world is a locked room,
no windows and no doors,
all of us inside
inhaling our neighbor's breath.

The world is a purple flower
in the wilderness of heaven,
fragrant and falling apart
alone in the killing dust.

                    1972

When the bus arrived in Tel-Aviv, I was struck by their sleep:
two men, thirtyish, dark skinned, dressed up in new
trousers, shirts, ties, everything gleaming
under their two well-cut blank profiles,
close to each other, a sculptured closeness,
their features unmistakably Hittite.

Then I knew that their whole festive rig
had grown on them without their realizing.
Sleepers for ninety generations, swept into the city at a gallop,
and opening their eyes now, amazed and briefly emboldened,
were about to crash unbridled into the dust of our lives.
And I knew we were braking, pulling into the Central Bus Station
where something horrendous would befall them.

## THE SECRET OF AUTHORITY

When in the inner sanctum a purple seal is stamped on papers
   sharp as razor blades whose size has gone haywire:
when telephone receivers are brandished like spears:
when they ring the bell, then bang the door with their fists:
when soldiers present arms and the executioner puts on his watch,

not only does the cow go on giving milk, not only does the chicken
lay unbroken eggs: a young
woman walks into the field and picks flowers
to fill her room with perfume, and a young
man goes to town, buys her a ring
with a red stone.
The jeweler touches the gold
and is transported. Across the road
the dealer in dry goods fondles muslin.
As for the butcher, he cracks bones
and then slices perfect cuts of meat.
His dog is strange: he's learned to watch his master patiently
for no raw meat.
From the laundry, steam always rises,
in the fish store they keep things spotless
and the lady from the housewares shop
is also a matchmaker: usually she gets around to
affairs of the heart in the evening, but sometimes
she has to put up a sign: Back Soon.

This sign's a field day for children returning from school:
they tie a dead rat to it,
stick a peach pit in its mouth.
When she comes back from her matchmaking, she faints and they
bite their fingers on the opposite roof.
When she recovers they're gone, no trace of them, just a big sun
making noon music
and a little girl singing, hoping to be a bird.

And the authorial I hears
a voice: Fine, very nice, and you,
what do you have to say?
What do I say? I too
drink milk, fry eggs in butter,
go from shop to shop and come back with some paper bags.
I listen to music at night.
Next to a woman I'm calmer.
The racket of kids consoles me for my death.
I empty my house of newspapers,
radio, television, all these
feeble striptease shows of social disgrace.
I don't lift a finger
against the hands that slap our intelligence,
I don't say a word
against the tramping that deafens the beat of the heart.

I see clearly, or so I imagine,
what's done in the inner sanctum, the placard faces
with nothing behind them
but a simple mistake in arithmetic.
I see the children turn into soldiers,
and the girl soldiers turn into mothers,
and the mothers weep and make their children into soldiers.
I see the line drawn on the map
and the line under the names of people in notebooks sealed in safes.
Reading about people who believed in redemption, I understand
they also miscalculated. But their error was different,
more godlike. Yes, here I'm getting down to God,
a painkilling drug, with its built-in damage.

## IN CAMERA

Until she came I danced alone
and danced alone until I heard
the click of her heels.

And when she came
I stopped. All the dance tracks in the room shrank to one stare.

She had forgotten to take off her face mask.

She went through town like that,
not taking it off.
She climbed the stairs like that, she rang the bell like that, she entered
    like that:

she bought, it turns out,
lots of expensive cosmetics
and now she's loaded with them.
She can arrange them all in a circle and stand in the middle and smile.

And the face mask
grips the smile
and serves it up with a clenched fist

And music, music
endlessly played in the background
doesn't know how to stop.

And I, who have stopped, begin to grow taller.
Soon the ceiling.
And my head will bump, will break through, will see

the whole town.
But not her.

Every arm
    is a potential stump
this potency
    lies in the threat
not always being realized.

    Its stumpness
doesn't come, never
        even
hours of lassitude pass
    or they're forgotten
so every arm

revolves around its joints
    activates
its crane-ness
    and sometimes
exquisitely;
    and all this time
medical books
    are filled with hideous pictures.

## SEALED IN A BOTTLE

*On reading Sasson Somech's* Anthology
of New Syrian and Lebanese Poetry
*(1973)*

This east bank of the Mediterranean
is hard on poets, hard on the vigilant word.
We are derelict nations, greedy for our own justice,
our slogans flap in the sea breeze every evening.
Our weapons are always at the ready.

Our politicians are quick to declare us
the Cradle of Civilization. Jerusalem, Tyre, Sidon.
Great Crib of Damascus. We've been rich in prophets.
We straggle behind a long historical caravan.
What are these bloody bandages around our wrists?
Why do our lips crack, and why do we spit like the plague stricken?
(My brother Shauqui Abi-Shaqra, my brother Muhammad Al-Maghut,
instead of cradle, we should read crypt,
Damascus, Tel-Aviv, Beirut, our crypt is snug.)

This east bank of the Mediterranean loosens
a light breeze at evening. From Latakia to Ashdod
this eastern basin is filled with
summer howling, watermelons.
And later, night like the black sleeve of an old camera.
On these legendary shores everything comes with a pedigree,
what a field day for tourists,
retired Americans, some Germans. Anyone

who's a fan of easy exotics—light on the stomach, no commitment
and on relatively favorable terms—can find it here.

Let's have a little night music now, with a communal masturbatory
   dream,
i.e.: a three-layer cake with thick cream and stale marzipan
for the 5734th anniversary of the Creation.

The town sinks under the weight of its own
siege, and markets fear.
Unemployed antiaircraft gunners
shoot at the full moon.

In the gray light of television
wives kneel in their sagging nakedness
and mummies of love slowly fill up
with juices like false pregnancies.

Furious blackout squads
whistle at them from the dark,
old men and the mobilized young
stone them with vulgar syllables.

They stare, wash themselves over and over
as though defiled by some obscure impurity,
and pace the room like whores
who got mixed up about the times,

or are terrified of time passing
sticky and gasping. They jump
to the window, return to the sofa
look for something, find nothing,

stretch out and kick aimlessly,
missing picture after picture.
Until the empty screen after midnight
lights their contracted thighs.

October 20, 1973<br>Tel-Aviv

A dull khaki light comes down again
in a dense, polluted cloud
against the gaping balconies
of our houses pitched in sand,

against the facial nerves that crave
relief from an autumn breeze,
faint shudder in a singed cheek,
a dull khaki light again:

a dull khaki light comes down again
against these fractured thoughts
on a taut elliptic form
we repeated in the sand,

and across the simple food
we spread under a tree
and gathered to eat with joy,
a dull khaki light again:

a dull khaki light comes down again
on glasses we filled with wine;
we leaned over living purple,
over last year's remembered taste,

to the plumlike breasts of girls
tucked lightly in loose cloth
catching the touch of a hungry wind
a dull khaki light again:

a dull khaki light comes down again
over our wounded love
on memories dissolving
we'll sort and lose in time,

on our flesh that's scheming to collapse,
on our clutch at a human shape
as a being that swallows and sees,

a dull khaki light comes down again

A burning cigarette tossed into a tree
at five o'clock in the morning
blooms for a minute in red brilliance among the leaves.

You might as well say it's the fruit of the tree
(tobacco, paper), a different tree
granted, but why be picky?
The fruit glows, the fruit fizzles out.

A man has his fill for a minute, then doesn't.

A heat wave in March already at five A.M.,
the temporary gold of sunrise flickers behind humps of houses.
Television antennae scribble
an awkward message in a primitive script.
The street's beaten gray still gives off a violet glow.
In a lighted window
a woman makes coffee and toast.
I can see spring has gone out of her shape.
Now I'll sleep.
I'll skip the peak hours.

I first came across the Bible
when I was a small child,
it was *The Illustrated Bible* by Doré.
There were visions, awful sights:
a king falls on his sword, a king
hurls a lance at a musician. A boy
brandishes a giant's severed head, a young man
rips a lion apart, cities tumble.
The Bible, it turned out, was a place full of spectacles
charged with tense and glorious horror.

Later I got to know the Bible through the Genesis stories,
I quickly discovered
The Bible was made of words:
light darkness water,
and it told about people overpowered
by the elements and a talking God.

Through torrents of words the human vessel sails.

And a long time passed before the prophets arrived.
They were already people
not unlike me, and God
had become a murmur
stylized by a young man from Tekoa or Anathoth.

Kings honored them
because a certain type of king respects audacity.
A limited extraterritorial status
was bestowed on them by the will of the people.

But a radical modernization of the human
was already taking place.
Political intrigue—calculated and blind—
decided the fate of the masses, exiled
along with the last divine stylists.

Now they performed in the sphere of the possible,
criticized, lamented, stirred a little hope.

## A DREAM OF DEATH AS AN ANGEL

People cloaked in linen robes
eating olives and sesame seeds
reading scrolls
in walled cities
in forests
on pillows on stones,

dreamed the day of their passing
in the shape of an angel who comes
from a wall or tree
the knife
in his hand
makes explanations superfluous.

They go with him they don't complain
or they ask wait awhile
till I make provisions
for my household
till I finish my job
then you'll lay your hand upon me.

And in special cases
found in the text
it's possible to negotiate with him
to say you're early
go and come back

in a couple of months, a year.
For even an Angel of Destruction like him
retreats when faced with a knock-down argument
with the truth of human life
nor does he dare
to presume
there's substance in what someone says:

he goes as he came
returns some other time
from the wall or tree
the gleaming knife
in his hand
shines like the heavenly spheres.

# ECOLOGY

I

Vase-shaped islands
dip in the Mediterranean
under a moon sailing out
on a Greek barge

Now with a green pencil
I am getting this down:
the sea is not very far
the past even closer

the future's transgressions will be
shaken from every pocket
feet immersed to the ankles
in the traditional *Tashlikh*

millions and millions of tires—
all discarded—will form
a bridge over the water
to New York from Gibraltar

a mountain of skeleton cars
will rise out of North Africa;
whoever sees it from Malta
will grab a flight to India

a huge Japanese lantern
will light up the island of Cyprus
this enormous paper accordion
will shriek until it rips

2

My wife is a Greek sea-goddess
it's clear to the ones who know her
ancient musical morals:
a cat swallows a crab

I'm Poseidon fleeing
the rage of my heart-empty brother
who hurls bolts of lightning
regardless of any offering

I have seen the hardness of things
heaps of ecological hazards
my seraphic siren turned
into a drowning cow

we are becoming fewer
our sea is also shrinking
our knowledge sails before us
and in its wake we follow

in an underwater convoy
we'll tour the country's beaches
nymph-like fishes wiggling
through sunken barbed-wire fences

this is a final warning
to all singing sea creatures:
there's certain death on the beach
on the beaches death is waiting.

I

Out of a glutted slumber I rise with a love of words
just as an old love suddenly wakes
to smooth out a crease in my memory.

And already I've said
on the run: form has turned into matter, soul into flesh.

And the flesh is trapped—
biology
history
narrative and death.

3

And history is a ragged uniform, discolored,
crusted with earth. Pure earth
without design,
or thought,
or intention,
                saves
seeds, powdered
bones, worms' eggs.

5   Good

It'll be good if I die and you survive me.
Someone who hasn't heard will come to look for me.

And you'll say, but he's dead. And he'll ask, of what?
Then you'll say: of his love
for the heaviness of earth.

8

I gave my dog an old sandal,
sole made of pressed cork and tough leather.
He's working it over—hard and thorough—
his jaw is very busy and his paws
maneuver within the limits of their dogness
while I'm sitting on the chair naked
except for shoes and socks on my feet,
sitting deep inside the night
trying to fish out one old scrap of sweetness
to sugar my last hour before sleep.

9

Not long after sunset
they close the shutters
turn off the lights
decree silence

they shut themselves in
against the night, lovely murderous summer night
that wanders through the streets
walking and crying

12    Naive Painting

The world created in the shape of a courtyard in South Tel-Aviv.
A wreck of a eucalyptus stands for the Third Day.
A hungry cat for the Fifth.
God on the right, in the image of an old Bukharan man in clean
    underwear
says unto the virgin Daughter of Israel,
a fifteen-year-old Yemenite, playing a tape deck loud on the opposite
    balcony:
please switch off the music
on the day the Temple was destroyed.
The ninth of Av is an ancient day of mourning for us Jews.
What does Yemima say?
She doesn't.
She turns up the volume.


13

A woman in black
on the street corner
her boy wears a black skullcap
she signals for a taxi
a long time passes
she takes the child's hand
crosses the street
she's not unattractive
her widow's clothing suits her

her legs are shapely in black stockings
somewhat transparent
her wrists very white in all that blackness
her face is beautifully fixed
between black hair and black shawl
evening comes
a long time has passed
she's still signaling

16

There are many words I haven't put down. Their flavor
absorbed in articles of clothing, accessories—mixed
with other people's breath—stained the walls.

Those words and their shattered combinations
returned unto dust the way
I too will return.

But they were words,
and could be rescued.

## LOVE POEM

Tarnished yellow is the color of dust
that covers the cities. On clear days
there's a white luster, on overcast days
a smoky gray. Allergic noses
stay safe behind locked windows,
closed shutters. Lines of cars
crawl feverish along melting roads. Dutiful
hands grip the padded steering wheels.
While flies take their siesta
air conditioners hum into hidden caves.
What's left of the grass is scorched in the yards.
Loaves of life burn in the earth's oven.

Extravagant brown hair
flares around your lovely head
all of it—skull eyes teeth
earlobes
lips

a listening flower
staring peach
blinking apple
nose-wrinkling nut
humming pomegranate
pondering pear
weeping orange

nibbling avocado
your floating head
tamed in bubbly shampoo.

I consider the word *affliction*
a word from a menacing book full of fathers
a word from my brain's mine shaft packed
with workers, tough men with a day's growth
clutching drills in hard hats and overalls.
The rest of my life I'll carve out one smile.

I consider the word *affliction*
a word wrapped in willow and affection.
Loaded with skeletons of beasts like rocks buried in sand.
Like flutes that unwittingly whimper a broken tune.
A word melting at dusk when the lights come on.
A wandering in my bones, mouth bitter and longing.

A rumpled white
sheet touches
your slumbering breast,
touches the unintentional
rise of your nipple.

## GARBAGE DUMP, 2000

I didn't like your faces from the start.
The words you spoke sounded phony.
Your plans were tiresome.
Even your women dreamed about something else.
But I carried on next to you day after day.
I simply had nowhere else to go.

Your futures looked doubtful to me.
Your fondness for your mistakes and your lies made me sick.
Your blindness wasn't even innocent.
Some appendage sprouted in you, bequeathed from a lower order of
    mammals.
But I kept finding myself in your company.
I was an orphan, completely broke.

I saw you polluting everything around you without restraint.
The most simple solutions you took as castles in the air.
Only desolation seemed simple and real enough to you.
Your children learned to growl in helpless agreement.
But I didn't turn my back on your company.
Somehow I learned to love and to hope.

My love and my hope had nothing to feed on.
Shadowy corners in the huge junkyard were all heat and rust.

Even the nights were thick and hazy.
Sated, sleepy faces displayed a vacuous denial of mortality.
But I made up my mind long ago this is where I'll end.
My body and soul have ripened as fruit of this dump.

# SALT ON THE WOUNDS OF THE LAND

1

A thin, honed wail
whirs at a low altitude
the level of car roofs
the level of girls' breasts

whirs over the street
barely misses my skull
in its usual place
in my chair at the café

2

I wasn't in Sachnin
I wasn't in Kafr Canna
I didn't throw stones
I didn't shoot into the crowd

I didn't set up checkpoints
I didn't seal locks
I didn't burn tires
I didn't kill anyone

3
Over a cup of coffee
I'm told by an American photographer

how they buried
the body at Kafr Canna

The coffin was carried around
afterward the corpse was seized
and they hoisted it through the streets
a boy with four gaping eyes

4
In my usual place
I'm reading newspapers
that value one weeping over another
not all blood is red for them

they'll go on
with their crafty dreams
their clever ideas
salt on the wounds of the land

because to them it's a sick joke
to ask how Sakhnin is doing
and it's a waste of time
to swallow the pain of Canna

5

On stupid white paper
I type, erase,
correct, copy
with the grief of a moldy mind.

Land Day, 1976

War is the continuation of politics,
and South Lebanon is the continuation of Upper Galilee:
Therefore it's all too natural for a state
to wage war in Lebanon.

Youth is the continuation of childhood,
and South Lebanon is the continuation of Upper Galilee:
Therefore it's all too natural for boys and young men
to shoot at each other in Lebanon.

Grave-digging is the continuation of the rabbinate,
and South Lebanon is the continuation of Upper Galilee:
Therefore it's all too natural for the Army Rabbinical Burial Corps
to dig fresh graves in Lebanon.

The Press is the continuation of idle blabber,
and South Lebanon is the continuation of Upper Galilee:
Therefore newspapers discuss with high solemnity
the achievements of the war in Lebanon.

Poetry is the opposite of statement
in South Lebanon as well as in the Upper Galilee.
Therefore what was stated is as good as unstated,
and again we'll wage war in Lebanon.

                                          1978

## EXIT TO THE SEA

Once there was a woman.
She was very old.
For seventy-five years
she'd lived in this world.

When she was seventy-six
she thought she'd had enough.
She threw herself into the sea
to drown in its troughs.

The sea is a billion years old
and doesn't care about us.
It can drown old women daily
without any fuss.

But people were alarmed
and pulled her back to shore.
In the municipal hospital
she got the finest care.

Now she's in a Home
where they keep the Elderly.
In vain she'd hoped to find
a way out in the sea.

The poet dressed up as an angel of god
reveals himself at the same time
to the wife of Manoah and the wife of Joseph the carpenter.

With pure diction and perfect composure
he announces the birth of the son,
scourge of the Philistines and healer of hearts.

Fortune-telling and love of truth
don't go to his head:
not a word about the pillars or the cross.

His voice is all bliss and his demeanor
won't gouge eyes out or flay the skin.

Dressed up as an angel he leans over these women,
sweetens their womb and puts aside
the bitterness of history.

FROM *Letters and Other Poems (1986)*

The fright of the soul, if you begin by pulling out all the stops,
is a slammed bird, a dove imprisoned in the space
between the tiles of a roof, fled there looking for respite, some shelter.
Now its rest is only a flapping from beam to beam
in the raised dust.
A hundred surrounding slots of light are deceptive, impassable,
the in-out passage has disappeared like all the simple passages in this
    world.
The shelter has become a snare.
From now on there's only the fright of the dove caught in the space
the little fool sought for her salvation.
That's how you are in your life, close to mine
which loathes salvation and doesn't seek shelter,
makes do with a ditch, someplace to crash from time to time,
to enter, to leave, sleep, observe,
to touch, or avoid. I'm an unbeliever,
I tremble and deny fright,
observe it with a cold eye like a sore on the skin,
a scorched field next to a green one,
a crushed cat not far from another
leaping—essence of being,
despair for example; despair that breathes and makes poems.

Your mouth is filled with cotton wool according to their custom,
not satisfied with the dust we'll soon eat,
extractors of superfluous gold from the shamed mouth.
But they can't extract the panicky stare of the dead.
And I am the identifier, oh yes I identify: this is my mother
winter born, winter corpse, mother.

Even then your body betrayed you, that first winter
on the great trek east from the besieged city,
in out-of-the-way railroad stations, among all the other mothers
and children of DPs screaming on top of the bundles.
Even then it betrayed you, withheld its milk, and you
panicky like the dead with the load of your heavy infant
(his impossible weight almost finished you in your ninth month)
growing lighter every day, every station of the flight.

The two of us survived many times in this life,
each of us alone, each in a separate flight.

If there were other worlds
our reunion wouldn't be that far off.
My hair already glints with steel like yours
and it's clear I look more and more like your father.
Oh there's so much we'll never get straight.
There are endless folds in the staring space of time.

In the shadow of run-down buildings, at odd hours
I'll recover the clues to your past with a skill
not much greater than yours reading my future,
but I won't complain or despair of your memory.
From now on we won't move away from each other, we'll come a little
    closer,

a thin and tentative closeness, and very one-sided.
But my hand in your illusory hand, I'll keep drawing near
to the beneficent ease of your smile flickering before my cerebral eye,
to the traces of truths you stored in disordered drawers
under crumpled letters, photographs, hairpins,
bunches of old jewelry, new medicine,
dried flowers from withered gardens:

the stuff of our lives is the gold of transience
poured down our warm throats thirsting for milk.

*It's the worm inside the jumping bean that makes it race*

JOHN ASHBERY

You've always claimed you are inarticulate, and you've avoided
    explanation:
you blamed it on a common aversion to needless clarification.
I've kept a friendly silence, a speck of truth with a bubble of pus,
while Tomorrow wiped the slate clean, teased, covered its tracks,
    jumped ahead of us:

coffee in the morning or a new shirt, drinks at night, flirting.
Anxiety shot put is a well-known sport and we can function without
    hurting
over questions too difficult. Is there no music under the sun?
Or long hikes, shade, a worried love for everyone.

Dogs and cats moderate a life, not to mention children, holidays, gifts:
we're all magicians in a pinch, producing a rabbit or a fish
in miniature: and Tomorrow jumps over the treetops like a parrot
    repeating our wishes.
Sometimes rooms, houses, entire streets say *amen* with us.

You don't have to believe in an afterlife to wear a horse's blinders.
Dreams are something else, and we study them with ripples of
    reminders,
apprehension slowly dissolves: the coffee is ready, the cake baked, and
    Tomorrow acts
like a band of wandering players: glad to insert our own bits into the
    given text.

A racket, but at the same time, quiet. Two men in a room, a brave light,
two palm trees in the window, a building at a mind-sobering angle. All
  this while
wide awake. Circling a text or a watercolor. There is something
  commanding,
trustworthy, and vital in brief exchanges, contours: to nourish without
  understanding.

Nothing more. Or to understand and hush up, to be wounded and shut
  up. A hodgepodge of claims,
withdrawals from the perceptible: from the possible: the fun and
  games:
scary seesawing concepts. Stop, I say, Stop! Give yearnings the sack.
Actions will become clear, almost disappear. Tomorrow, jumping, will
  break its back.

In the shadow of absence I see
you curled soft and snug
on your side, wrapped in the coat
of somebody else (I broke
with her too), a familiar smile
trickling, delicate as loss.

Now, as before,
you won't say a thing, won't talk.
Eyes lit up, a naive hope of stealing
a shirt from Lafayette. An opaque world
rustles and raps
when you flare up at night,

a world full of mounds
over half-buried palaces, fine lattices
blocked with earth. Dreams
do not betray us, first we
betray them, so we can wake
tricked out like practical monsters, rich with ingenuity.

I'm back in the street where I haven't walked for ages
the sidewalk scattered with twisted human
heads screaming or sleeping
I go on walking as if nothing's wrong.
Newly dressed limbs wave from the shop windows
sway blindly and tap at the glass;
cars plow the roads going nowhere
just circling around themselves
in a constant despairing screeching of brakes
dogs locked and abandoned in some of the cars
struggle to force their muzzles between the glass and the frame.
Trees wave thousands of thumbtacked notes to herald events
already forgotten: the lost are now found, apartments rented.
And the tree where I passed out once and folded up
like an umbrella, knocking my head against the trunk—
it's worn out now, pitted and pocked by nails and tacks;
someone has ripped off all the notes.
Tiny rubber guitars are displayed in the shoe store,
colored tacks for the trees in the flower shop. A former gas station
transformed into a glass aerobics palace: women
of all ages moving with intense concentration, each locked
in herself, but no, they're all really projected onto a screen
from two small peepholes: the palace is a superstore
for a new generation of computers,
word processors. Acrid smoke rises
from the corner bookstore, but the books aren't consumed;

it's only smoke from *yahrzeit* candles
commemorating the founders. From the café next door
Arab boys dash out
with beat-up pink and green plastic buckets,
pouring over the sidewalk and gutter
puddles of blood and vomit,
that's what it looks like, but I don't stop to find out.
I go on walking as if everything's fine.
The pharmacy is closed at this hour, and so is the bank
that once was a grand café, two stories high,
full of cakes and a lingering fragrance of love;
but the old man in the faded kiosk still stands there
over his jars and yellowing
newspapers fastened by clips
he hasn't aged at all
looks like he hasn't even changed his vest,
only his eyes are gone
in their place are two tiny mirrors,
where my reflection is visible
against flickering traffic lights.

P.S.

His talking cat sits on the counter.
He was about to open his mouth,
but I shut him up
with a nod of my head. I know
his text: you are all slaves
to statistics, like your forefathers, slaves to theology.

## CITIES ON THEIR MOUNDS

Let's go back thirty years: the sandhill
at the edge of the lots was called a mountain. Shrubs,
hard and stubborn, held it together.
Nobody could name them.
When winter came wild daisies
and poppies sprouted, and edible *khubeiza*.
The mountain sat on two tracts of land
A tractor was hired to shave off the mountain. An instant
neighbors' quarrel, Our neighbor refused to pay his share.
There were outbursts in Yiddish, shoulder shrugs, fingers to foreheads.
The tractor driver lit another cigarette and pissed on the mountain.
The women tried to mediate without success. My heart
was split between the tractor and the mountain.
I wanted to see the tractor's wonders and wanted the mountain to stay
     put.
In the end I got both. The tractor sliced away half the mountain.
The remaining half grew taller before my eyes.
The vertical cut turned it into a cliff.
Slashed roots, quivering in midair, wriggled out of the cliff.
Hard sand was exposed under the soft.

Right there, with the two Katz brothers from down the road
I built my first city.
At the foot of the cliff we cleared the soft sand, and worked with the hard.
The hard sand was also brittle and treacherous.
We carved walls and mud huts, pressed lanes.

A spade and a wedge for the rough work, and popsicle sticks for details.
Chips of wood and eucalyptus bark became joists and gates.
In the heart of the city we erected The Temple of the Ape.
A crouching ape the size of a large baby,
the space between his legs the gate to a subterranean tunnel
the depth of our forearms. The entrance to the temple was blocked
by a lattice gate, chips of wood wrapped in tinfoil.
Menachem Katz sharpened the ape's teeth with the small blade of my
    pocketknife.
I stuck two halves of an orange Hanukah candle in the eye sockets.
At night, we lit the candles and kerosene torches on the watchtowers.

After a couple of days we waged war on the built-up city,
advanced on it with great force armed with slingshots and catapults.
We shot burning paper balls into it,
condemned it to hunger and horror.
The dumbfounded ape almost beat his sandy chest.
His invisible priests whined at his feet.
Avram Katz cast the first stone at him.
The lattice gate caught fire and the silver foil blackened.
Then the southern wall caved in.
But the city defended itself, a secondary wall
was quickly piled up to face the breach.
Like all besiegers in world history, we too had to eat supper.
The city breathed with relief and the ape's eyes shed paraffin tears.

Since then, I've built many cities
out of airier material; I've also invaded them.
With eyes closed and wide awake
I erected invisible kingdoms, followed their populations
and wandered through realms as they revealed themselves.
Generations of construction, generations of neglect, generations
of restoring and patching. Sometimes a generation shakes
    itself up,
as if everything starts again, runs for a while,
lays tiles that fit perfectly. What symmetry
suddenly runs the world! But the world
of one or two generations is just the skin of the milk
on top of the mass slowly souring below
thanks to the cunning of matter.
Cunning that do-gooders and designers of the future
detest so much.
This mass undoes symmetry, and if you look closer,
it's symmetry that goes wrong from the start; because of its amazing
    tension
something within symmetry breaks. I, too, unleashed havoc
to smash the airy maze,
to grant what was doomed to fall
its most fervent wish.
After that comes remorse—and the budding need to build on the
    mounds.

There is no building like building on mounds. To construct on the
    shattered,
used-up, and ruined
that are exposed again. Every connection
someone made here before speaks to you
in a connecting language. If there's enough remorse, enough ripening.
And if you've got it in you again—the calm and the restlessness of the
    builder,
the city under construction will build itself as it builds you.
Digging a ditch, someone finds a woman's head.
A queen, perhaps a goddess. He has no temple, no dynasty,
only a small garden. He hauls the head away in a wheelbarrow
padded with a sack, sets it
on a rock some distance from a tree.
A young tree, shadeless. He plants
flowers around the rock from some other place.
The tree's shade is a thing of the future. Even now twilight comes,
the woman opens her eyes, begins to talk.
It seems as though whatever she says
was put in her mouth by someone before you, a dead man. But no,
she speaks from your throat. You wonder at the lyrics, her voice also
is new. But you'll get used to it, you'll pull yourself together.
While you are talking, the tree gives shade,
you too are dead. But you both go on talking
as equals. The flowers spread their fragrance,
human footsteps keep coming.

## PRO & CON

I can't stand political poetry: that civil or prophetic posturing
(Why should a citizen speak in broken lines?)
or the irony of paper fighter planes facing steel and bulletproof glass
    and the elephant stampede
of the electorate and the elected.
It's disgusting, the glory of bamboo arrows versus dive-bombers
or, just as bad, that prophetic stance:
ventriloquism in the name of History, the facile analogies, truisms,
master plans for redemption. Quiet!
Let's have some quiet here—
let the poet turn inward, let him study his navel,
dream of his father and mother,
or draw the pigeons on the neighbor's roof—
a street in the city, a house on the street,
a room inside the house, an orange peel on the table
slowly
drying.

Just not that spectacle:
someone on edge picks up the morning paper,
listens to news on the hour, follows
the TV broadcasts—and by late evening is ready to hold forth
(render unto the politician what belongs to Caesar, and unto the jour-
    nalist what belongs to his eunuch).
Just not that spectacle. And above all,

quiet. Quiet, I say.
Let there be quiet here.

But sometimes I can't control myself, and like a pervert
I sneak up on the wax figures' display.
Here they are, lined up in a row, those gawky masks in charge
of deciding our fate in these times.
They are posed with the postures of men who get things done,
they sit skewed by the weight of responsibility,
smiling their smiles almost like humans
or earnestly staring with molded expressions.

And I emerge into the coolness of lampposts,
a street, locked shops,
look at a flicker in the glass.
Light and free. Cold and hot.
Here and not.
Blood and rot. Snot
I say, snot-shot.

## SONNET: AGAINST MAKING BLOOD SPEAK OUT

If I die one day from the bullet of a young killer—
a Palestinian who crosses the northern border—
or from the blast of a hand grenade he throws,
or in a bomb explosion while I'm checking the price
of cucumbers in the market, don't dare say
that my blood permits you to justify your wrongs—
that my torn eyes support your blindness—
that my spilled guts prove it's impossible
to talk with them about an arrangement—it's only possible
to talk with guns, interrogation cells, curfew, prison,
expulsion, confiscation of land, curses, iron fists, a steel heart
that thinks it's driving out the Amorites, destroying the Amalekites.
    Let the blood seep into the dust; blood is blood, not words.
    Terrible—the illusion of the Kingdom in obtuse hearts.

## CONVERSATION WITH A RADIO

                    Without blushing
my radio sings: *A song I dreamt about Prague.*
Radio radio, I say,
aren't you ashamed—singing
about Prague right now.
Can't you sing anything else?

It's August, the radio says,
time to mark the loss of freedom
in Czechoslovakia, shock troops,
tanks on the streets—have you forgotten?

Of course we're in August, I agree,
August '82. An August like no other.
Who needs your commemorations,
sentimental crap about the loss of freedom,
someone else's, somewhere else.
Prague is *bobkes* next to Beirut
(I'm trying to talk to my radio in its own language),
your song is piffle,
when you talk, you lie.

I'm just a radio, he says,
I'm a mouthpiece, not a mouth.
I can broadcast greetings,
quote our sources, our informants,

send out speeches and songs for holidays,
holy days, memorial days
I run on reruns.

What do you want from me?
You call this lying?
Don't embarrass me with the truth.
Come on, don't be fooled
by a little electronic sophistication:
I'm more primitive than a toothless, illiterate
old Palestinian woman.

And I have to agree.
I'm the one who should be blushing.
Who said I should start talking
to an electronic system with nothing behind it
but the common wish to be deceived yet righteous?

## SOLILOQUY OF DADA THE CAT

I was scrawny as a wormy branch
going wild in trash cans, and I was a pampered pet
stuffed with prime turkey to restore me, and then again
I was a beloved kitty fattened with a baby bottle,
and I was a neglected cat, kicked down the stairs or out into the yard,
revived. Once more I was mad
with desire, seized by insatiable lust, fucking
not eating, always on the prowl, moaning in heat,
all skin and bones from my gaping libido.
And once again, later, a stay-put cat
rubbing against the family, greedy for petting, a glutton
about to explode. I'd roll on my back and my fats would gurgle.
I'd curl up on fine couches or under parked cars
finding some warmth in puddles of oozing black oil. I ate
trash can mash, roast duck, and fried liver. Fought over
a filthy margarine wrapper, turned up my nose at rich soup.
Was kicked and got up, degenerated and survived.
And went on fighting. Followed my family from one neighborhood
to another, refuting the rumor that cats are fickle,
loyal to places and not to people. I was different
and paid for it seven times over with mangled fur. Gave up being
pampered, domestic, and dug my teeth hard in the kings of alleys,
staked my claim to new territory and scared away bullies.
I walked around slashed, punctured by wounds, infections, and pus.
And recovered again, with some thin scattered scars.

I was an innocent young tom besides, courtly and generous, kept a
    she-cat
on a corner of the roof for a while and shared my food with her.
I'd also daydream, lying in wait for pigeons on the ledge.
Whole days dreaming, pouncing for nothing, dreaming.
Sometimes I'd be an odd friend of the pet dog
who'd take my head gently in his mouth and drag me around in a
    zigzag.
I wouldn't resist. Other times I'd be half a tiger, far removed
from dog or man. Or else I'd be sorry,
let anyone roll me over in his arms,
scratch and massage my fat belly (I'd get fat again
and only pretend to bite).
Nothing surprises me anymore,
about myself or anyone else. They say a cat has nine lives.
Maybe more. I've been low as the lowest, high as the highest,
sick in every sense of the word. Even then I recovered.
I can be startled from my lair, not much more.
The world still goes on,
no small wonder, no surprise. I am what I am.

A discriminating hand
hovers over the keyboard
         no longer
treats it like a page of bond paper
or a small electronic piano     this hand
of someone who going by age
could be my son or yours
but in truth is the grandson of, say,
a tailor from Romania,
puts together words
signs      makes a great
effort
not to represent the shoulder
the elbow or pelvic bone
not even the brain
rocking
in the skull's darkness somewhere above it
coaxes it
to favor the signifier
over the signified     so does
this brain fantasize its trip through
black space     forgets
or doesn't remember that never
was there ever a signifier born
in this world except
from a foolish love for the deferred signified

the blind the dark
for example the love of the hand for the foot
the desire of the brain for the buttocks
warm blood for scattered dust
the hungry for the bread's flesh
the scoundrel for his god.

## CHEESE

We live in an age when it's hard
to write about basic things
like a kiss or eating cheese.
Not that it was ever easy. They were so few, so rare, in fact,
in every generation. So that when you blew off the dust
only a few pages would escape the bony fingers
of theology, ideology,
or at least
some wild desire for life everlasting,
immortality of the soul or the page.
Yes, this is the poet's wooden leg,
the ripening hope
that slippery paper will outlive bronze.

Cheese outlives nothing.
Cheese, a small, soft cake of it, is a very appropriate noun
to put with the adjective "rotten."
Not to mention a kiss you could only
pretend to contain in a square
or triangle of being, like cheese,
so much is it totally blended
with the stir that precedes it, with the motion
that follows, releasing the bodies.
It has no ego, even its shape
is suggested only by the gymnastics
of the neck and the body from the waist up

—these are its levers,
but at the same time it lights a fuse in the loins,
and the true kiss
is recorded in the invisible frenzy
of a thousand particles of blood
all at once in the body.
That's why poets forsake the cities and flee
and the Philistines come and dwell in them.

## MUSÉE PICASSO, OR SOME WORDS IN PRAISE OF HUMAN FOOLISHNESS

Our formulations make it difficult
to honor human foolishness properly, though nothing else
is worthy of homage, love, endearment.
Our great wisdom brings us
to burned cities, smoldering heaps
of scorched iron, corpses rotting in the sun
or in unceasing rain
that we, children of wicked astonishment,
interpret as metaphor
for blessing.

But foolishness, our human advantage,
brings us at least a night of wet dreams,
performs for us, upside down under eyelids
that simulate sleep, the kisses, embraces, and whispers
we've lost and will soon lose again,
the precious encounters we've squandered,
sweet nothings we've heard or we might have heard.
And still we act foolishly, sail toward tomorrow
trading expected encounters for unattainable happiness,
though even the seed of a wrecked happiness sweetens
the life still pumping in our sensitive parts.

How sweet and delicate is human foolishness.
It keeps tossing our way
such amazing glissandos to surprise us

out of our crumpled hideout, to bounce us
into a new acquaintance with foolishness shining
from our seemingly open eyes. And thereby
hangs a tale:

Someone who thinks he's wise goes
on a summer day to a place frequented by ones in the know,
e.g., a museum. Light-footed, he walks with a clear purpose
and around the next corner finds the familiar structure,
the gate he's to enter. But before he steps into that place
where skill and dead genius blaze in a flame forever,
foolishness hugs him and there out of nowhere presses his mouth
with hot wet kisses. The way a small child creates
a world out of used matches. Or jackets, in our case.
A car stops beside him like a UFO, and a young man
from Calabria with a silvery calling card from a leather shop in Rome
cons him with an arabesque tale about his terrible disaster,
how he came to Paris to sell his goods and managed quite well
till he was screwed by French crooks who picked his pocket in a
    Montmartre bar
and left him with two last jackets in his car and no wallet,
not to mention no gas for the drive home and not a soul he could turn
    to in Sodom.
What luck, maybe Santa Maria sent you to me, what luck
that my designer eye sees at once how these two jackets fit you to a T

as if tailored for you, as if you came to me in a dream,
and I, who wanted nothing but a few gas refills for the car, a baguette,
    and some cheese,
so I can reach Rome alive and well, I'm dying to give these to you as a
    gift
free of charge, that is for 1,400 francs instead of 10,000, their real value.
Because you deserve it, the minute I set eyes on you I knew:
here's the first real man in this city of skunks
who's got light in his eyes, who won't throw me to the dogs.

On the stairs to the museum, in the middle of a summer day, wrapped
    in the coolness of human wisdom
and inspiration, the wise one stands at the end of this tale holding a
    plastic bag
with one useless jacket, for which the Calabrian got 350 francs, since
    that's all there was
Not much of a deal, but pleased to drive off and look for another
    sucker.

But that's not the point, and this whole story is just
a kind of parable, more like a comma. And it's not even
the end of the story which doesn't have or need an end.

Above the antique restored structure, remodeled for its present
use to store the signs left by one man

in a lifelong struggle, stubborn and hopeless,
against the absence of meaning, against death,
now rises the immaculate angel of foolishness with outstretched
wings, waving a foolish jacket,
blessing it and you and me,
AMEN
amen.

Paris
July 1991

## BURNING HOLY BOOKS

Holy books, said my friend, angry,
there's no such thing. Books,
books: let them talk
to us about books.
It was a hot night.

    At noon light rips
through the room, and everything's clear:
over the holy we'll put a transparent
grid. From now on we'll examine it
with a critical eye, we'll see
the holy, crisscrossed through bars:
iron or a mathematical passion.

Will this make it look less
holy? Now it's evening.
It could be a mistake,
our own.

But the grid should be placed there. With courage,
with care. It's time to preserve
the wreck of holiness.

*from Windows Near Mallarmé*

LIVE

Why do you live as if the world
were shaking with fear?
The world isn't afraid to die.

## THE HEAD

Scattering words like seeds
to sprout meaning in the shifting ground of what is,
the head is a thickening of the one that would bury itself
between smooth hills that shivered in a bluish aura of veins,
moving its lips to grope for sleepy happiness
in a region of sweet slaking.

Is a thickening of the one that threw itself in the lap
of a dress like a puppy, sniffing the strong-smelling flesh
that cradles the fetus, the linkage,
painkiller for the living mammal, terrified
by the inanimate, by insects, by fish, by fowl.

## WINDOW TO THE FUTURE

In laced-up boots the nineteenth century
steps down from the carriage onto the stone pavement
covered with the fish market filth.

Her hand holds a portable brass telescope
her pocket silver coins with the emperor's profile
and her heart the dream of flying like a bird.

On the syphilis ulcer a mousseline hankie
(in the distance the broken groan of a coal locomotive)
in the brain the roar of the chorus from Antigone.

Soon the hieroglyphs will be deciphered
ah, to what end
and dust from Mars will be heaped on the desk.

# RIVER IN THE DESERT

You stand at the window combing your hair,
blank face of someone on trial.
Houses between us collapse. I see you
innocent, a mare's startled blink.
*The mane of your hair is a lukewarm river,*
I will translate for you, *where, not shuddering,*
*the Soul that gives us nightmares will be drowned.*
Do you get it? And then *there will be*
*a nothingness, a total stranger to you.*

*The two of us will never be one mummy buried*
*under cheerful palm trees in an ancient wilderness.*
Summer, grieving, will swoop down on the city.
At night the clanging and buzzing will die down.
Almost completely. Out of a window the scream
of a living sleeper. A car runs over it.
Only in dreams can we walk unblemished, and entwined,
our bare skin veiled with a film of salt and sand,
facing a wounded mango sun at the end of day.

## THE FOWL OF THE AIR

The paper boat was tossed in the puddle,
the lake filled with birds,
and a bird plucked off her redundant wings
tore off her beak and licked the blood
from her open wound, her newborn lips. At last,
she said, I've arrived. Smells of scorched grass,
leftover thorns, smoldering earth, a faint trickle
of water at body temperature. The pale glitter
through the haze is the sun, said the bird.
I'll go to work, there's a city to build
and a tower, heading for heaven.

# THE FLOWER OF ANARCHY

It had an amazing scent, the anarchic flower—
when I was young it flashed out of books and genealogies
and with a hand eased by the thwack of hope
I offered it to the world and you

the world bit my hand,
but you and I kissed

The flower bloomed from the machine of blood and death
splendid and true as a waking dream
like you growing lovelier day by day
when it faked immortality you laughed and trembled

I embraced you
but didn't sleep nights

Our fragrant orphanhood did not last
its programmed wilting grew like an embryo
and the great wind of anarchy blasted the roof
off whatever you thought would shelter our love

the world smiled at us  why not
we didn't even cry

We moved through gardens savage with fruit
up in the trees, parrots repeated our promises

wounds smiled at us openmouthed like flowers
and all we wanted was a white repose on a bare mountain

you looked back
and I became a snowman

The flower of anarchy still sways in the summer wind
leaning bodies smell of memories that make them dance
and dreams sneak in at night with a whisper to sweeten
the hard waking in the crowded city

no snow where we live
and we're still smiling

## THIN LIVESTOCK

Mounted on goats and rams
(even on roosters)
we will enter the city that used to be our city
(we'll be so light
that thin livestock will carry us easily)
we will advance along the strange streets
past entrances of abandoned houses
where we kissed on the doorsteps
strong sweet kisses.
Long-vanished coffee shops will flash
their pastries never-to-be-baked again,
their smell still lingering.
Through ordinary squares, through gardens
programmed with computerized drip systems,
we will move in an abject procession
insulting the good taste
of other generations,
even their sense of justice.

# FAR FROM THE FLAG PARADE

It was sweet, dark, and tangy
under the heavy branches
of the citrus trees bent
around Ein-Hatkhelet and Avikhail.
I called it homeland.
Shade streaming from the tree,
the heavy heads of the Shamutti oranges
scattered around me,
a glowing, saturated yours-for-the-taking,
far from the flag parade,
I called it homeland.
That was a long time ago. A kind of piratical act
of a boy who found
something he wasn't looking for.

1    Bitch/Armchair

The springy bitch is coiled
in the curve of the armchair: her carved head
tucked between two dangling paws,
her slanted canine stare, alert, on the prowl
for what's coming.

          You need to shape
the contrast between the rigid
legs of the armchair
and the legs of the bitch
at ease, folded over,
lying low for a gigantic leap,
a hind let loose in open fields,

             or sharpen
the alert and dreamy flicker
in her round eye, its hidden
wordless cerebration, and yet all
readiness to meet your eyes,
to snuggle, follow after.

A bitch in the curve of the armchair,
a foot in a shoe,
an eye in the forehead,
spellbound breathers in the philosophic cave—

but I'm no painter.

3   Death thought/Dog sprints

The dog sprints sideways at an acute angle
his wide nostrils quiver without guile
he sniffs the secrets of the dry grass
and his fluttering ears
are banners celebrating
a disregard for death.

Come with us dog, we humans
built a fire in the pitch dark
of a universe bleating with ignorance
and found in its light
the hidden secret of all life
the day of death flickering on the horizon
a self-creating mirage
that suddenly materializes
into a certainty we cannot reach
but we'll be swallowed in, and then dissolve.

Come with us, we who have sowed
death to the four winds scorched
scalded and suffocated
this globe floundering in the cosmic dark
know now: death is the father of brotherhood.

## RAINY LOVE

*after Pablo Neruda*

You are still flickering in the fading light of the universe,
my furtive guest, fugitive from the rain
holding a tulip dripping water.
What have you to do with this white head clasped
each day between my hands like a pale gourd.

The wind growls, bangs on the shuttered window,
now the sky is a heavy net, swarming with shadows of fish.
The rain rips off your clothes and lets them drop,
birds wheel in fright. But in here the wind
finally calms down.

Out there it blows, barking, growling.
But the storm ignores us,
whirling heaps of blackening leaves,
scrambling shapes defined all morning in the sun.
I don't fight it out, not even with humans.

You are here, you do not run away, clinging
as if impelled by a violent fear. But not of me.
To me you hand the stalk of your body like a flower,
and your small breasts smell like a field of clover.
But an invisible shadow hovers over your eyes.

Now you are not like anyone else, slowly
we'll fall in the quiet garden of sheets.
Your presence drifting from one decade to another

will be absorbed by what spread before you were born.
Afterward I'll smoke, and your name will be scribbled in smoke.

Outside, the unrelenting wind slaughters butterflies,
and I shiver in a flight of love and joy
swallow the brimming plum of your lips,
shake your belly and forget my name. Until it bursts
from your mouth in a final cry.

But awake, your dream of adjusting to me
will cause you terrible suffering.
My soul, that seems to you so perfected,
is a solitary, big-boned predator,
and I shed leaves like a tree in the wind.

We've watched dawn scrape the sky,
kissing our eyelids, a gray light
brushing the window, and words, many words,
my mouth's murmurings, stroked the pale skin
of your curled body through nights of love. And I,

I could almost believe you were the universe in miniature.
But what did I give you? Flowers, chocolate, and kisses.
In the end you'll run away from me, far back
into the arms of that arid life
you hate so much, you say.

when a motorcycle turns over on its rider's back
and horns rip through the street
birds fly off in panic
and the cat hides at the far end of the courtyard
the typist makes it with her boss
and a small-time operator clinches a deal with an assistant
the fringe Ecstasy dealers hit the road
and the fitness club fills up with weight-losers

A man sits at a scratched piano
in a middle-sized room with closed shutters.
He is playing.
He is playing slowly.
The instrument is damaged but tuned.
He has no score in front of him.
The room is almost empty.
It has a bed, table, lamp,
sink, and refrigerator.
And in a corner
a dusty pile of scores.

when the car thieves scorch the road
and the policemen play backgammon
phone-tappers change cassettes
and cats pick at the garbage

a handyman pastes wallpaper in a sex-joint
a convict knifes his cell mate
the movie is over the audience spills out
and the party is about to start

He plays for the sake of playing
phrases he never played before
and won't repeat tomorrow.
They immediately melt away.
For a moment the body obeys.
The fingers rise and fall.
Memory switches off.
The spiderwebs of the brain
spin slowly around him.
You could say: he masturbates
as a way of life.

when thieves sneak back to bed
an unseen raven shreds the silence
a car reverses fast into a no-entry street
and a lone man dawdles on his way to pray
a moist woman laughs in her dream
a long-suffering worker bangs the garbage cans
a baby whimpers and then gives up
and the newly dead stiffens

The man sits at a scratched piano
and plays. The instrument quivers under him.
His back bends
or straightens slightly.
His lips murmur something.
His fingers are quick and springy.
His head light and hollow.
Playing lifts him like a wave
toward a jagged foggy shore.
That's where we'll leave him now,
slip away, and close the door.

Jerusalem, the Lord God's stone bench—
But the Lord God does not sit there.
A Muslim dealer in beans
sits on the pale stone bench.
Barely, on half his butt.
A plump nun is sitting there too
on the Lord God's stone bench. She's dreaming,
has been instructed to dream, of her sacred betrothal
to a crucified Jewish scholar. She too on half a butt.
But in the middle, with manifest pleasure,
feet spread wide, sits Ehud Olmert.
On his right knee he balances a bearded doll
(a Hassid in *capote* and *shtreyml*, passed down
from the Pale in Poland), on his left knee
a statuette of Astarte (a replica) from the Israel Museum.
He carries a gun too, but the flap of his jacket
covers it. The Hassid and Astarte aren't on speaking terms.
The merchant grinds his teeth, but his manners are good,
he nods *Shalom*. The nun—she too mumbles
*Shalom, Shalom*. So does Olmert.
His butt feels cold, but his heart is warm,
he smiles from ear to ear.

Beautiful and virtual—
that's the Tel-Aviv Subway.
Bizarre, sprawling far
through a vastness that pinches our hearts.
Buried in mountains and valleys
she glows inaudibly,
our one-of-a-kind dream train,
flies incandescent in blood-red,
in asphalt-black, in concrete-gray,
and an airy opaque white,
the ancient color of human bones.
Because she was pieced together
out of odd parts:
reinforced concrete from fortifications,
Jerusalem stone, bypass roads,
red roof tiles, human bones.
Bones of our brothers, our children, bones of our cousins.
That's us, and that's the Tel-Aviv Subway
we dreamed of, united for, dedicated ourselves to.
Perhaps this secret subway of ours
spreads out a little too thin
over sites evacuated in the Sinai desert, over the splendid hills
that roll between Jenin and Hebron.
Some naysayers might claim it's too hard

to fit an escalator
in a subway like that.
So what? She's ours,
and there's no other like her on earth.

The Genoa-Rome train slows down, Rapallo.
Some fences, then the platform's edge, we stop.
Nothing special. A drowsy station, a few benches
shaded by low trees, a long brick wall.
The first houses are very close, laundry hanging
in a backyard blown almost onto the platform.
The sea is also close, patches of blue
between the quiet houses. And already moving on,
a bay appears in all its simple timelessness, dusky
blue water, dusky green woodland sloping down. That's it,
we're on our way south. A tunnel, and everything's gone.

So here, in one of the houses on a hillside,
lived that man: year after year, with the women
who cared for him. Reclusive, walking on the beach,
withdrawn. Tall shadow of a stem against the sea.
He's not to be pitied. It wasn't his fate that was hard on him,
he was hard on his fate. And what if he said,
I did not understand. I did not know, I understood nothing.
That's something, true, but a little vague.
This, of all things, was much too weak, admit it.
Shrunk, *sans élan.*
Time runs on, everything's on the move, cultures are treacherous.
They hardly read you today, you know.
Pretty soon only Jews will remember you,
unfavorably. Only the Jews. Jews have a grudging memory,
stuffed with bitterness. That's how it is now.

In the Jewish paradise they eat kreplach.
In the Russian and Ukrainian paradise
they eat kreplach too. Mongolians eat
kreplach. So do the Chinese
and the Japanese, who take special care
that the dough is extra-thin, transparent.

Jews and Pravoslavs say a blessing
over the kreplach, telling their god:
Blessed art thou for choosing us
of all peoples to feed on kreplach.
I have no idea what the Mongolians say.
The Chinese and Japanese also think
they are the chosen people. But not by gods.
To them, they pay their dues with a handful of coins.

Two helicopters kissed midair.
Out of that kiss fell seventy-three corpses.
One minute earlier they were young men ready for action,
carrying out orders as well as they could,
in full combat gear according to the latest standards,
belted to their seats as required,
equipped with cell phones and pocket money,
soldiers in an army that practices concern,
sons of anxious parents, proud
of their kids who volunteered
for the national mission, the famous fifteen-year-old mission
to launch a balloon known as Peace for the Galilee
by sending them off to the killing fields of Lebanon.

All this is hot air, empty rhetoric
that could just as well be dished out in opposite clichés.
Like a bunch of statistics about operational accidents and their lessons,
or a stiff-lipped national growl,
or well-rehearsed phrases re the unity of a nation in mourning,
or flower wreaths and speeches over a fresh grave multiplied by
    seventy-three.
But more than a thousand plus seventy-three corpses in this sector
in a preplanned war of forty-eight hours i.e. fifteen years,
and thousands of wounded disabled shell-shocked and fucked up
whose exact numbers are known only to some remote computer
    program in AKA—

all these corpses and wounded and disabled are so real
that any rhetoric is beyond them, their lives are finished,
even their likely screams have faded somewhere in Lebanon.

A war does not drop from the sky just like that,
it springs from the guts of a think tank rich in vision.
The takeoff of the helicopters is preceded by the takeoff of the creative
    idea
to kill seven flies with one decisive blow.
That's a rarefied idea, all spirituality, brilliance, and intelligence reports,
with no ovaries, no uterus, not one drop of semen.
But the corpses now collected in the military funeral parlor
will be distributed by the end of the day to private holes. And from
    there,
discreetly scattered in an infinite irreparable dispersion.
So now let's move on to a string of sad songs in a special broadcast all
    night, all day.
We've got the technology, no need to ask
if the singer is ready to sing. The tapes are waiting.
They will easily resound from the Dead Sea to southern Lebanon.

                                                    February 5, 1997

# A MARCH FOR LONG-DISTANCE POETS

Brother, the Muse hid tumbling
under the spiderwebs
in libraries slowly crumbling,

in spaces where whatever capers
could be the glittery eye of a mouse
feeding on crumpled papers.

When she passed, tapping discreetly
on high heels, naked
and pale as polished ivory,

a small voice stirred
through the slats of dusty shutters,
tickled a child's eardrum, was heard.

The believer in what words can do
believes in what they did to him. He who has climbed
steep wordy slopes
to the top of a cliff or descended
into dark caverns while
clutching their brittle projections
and imagining he'd find in their crevices
a mystic illumination,
the face of God, or hear
voices of the dead or voices
of the not-yet-born,
stands on the embers of words
and is silent.

"Abraham," page 10

    lines 8–9, **if you go right:** From Genesis 13:9.

    line 10, **a get-rich scheme:** From Genesis 14:23.

"Take a Look at My Rebels," page 11

    line 3, **Yokhanan of Gush-Halav,** and line 4, **Shimon of the Desert** (or Shimon Bar Giora): They both led the Jewish rebellion against Roman rule in 66–70 C.E.

"The Journey of the Great Egyptian Obelisk to the West," page 19

    line 51, **Nabulioon:** Arabic pronunciation of Napoleon.

    line 53, **Faranji:** Colloquial Arab word that was used for Frenchmen and Europeans in general.

"Adoshem," page 41

    title: Orthodox Jews are forbidden (except in prayer) to pronounce God's "real" names, one of which is *Adonai,* literally, "my Lord(s)," itself already a euphemism for YAHWEH. In conversation some say *Adoshem* instead. *Shem* is the Hebrew word for "name."

    line 18, **matzo:** According to one legend, when the Children of Israel left the land of Egypt in haste, they couldn't stop to bake their bread. So they carried the raw dough on their backs, and it was baked, without rising, in the sun.

"Sealed in a Bottle," page 54

    line 12, **My brother Shauqui Abi-Shaqra, my brother Muhammad Al-Maghut:** Names of Syrian poets represented in Somech's *Anthology.*

    line 27, **5734:** The Jewish calendar is lunisolar, with months calculated according to the moon, years according to the sun. It begins with the first year of the Creation.

"Wives of October," page 56

> title: The title and the date at the end of the poem refer to the war in October 1973, when Israel was suddenly attacked by Syria and Egypt on the Day of Atonement, and all the eligible men were called up to serve in the army.

"The Illustrated Bible," page 62

> line 22, **Tekoa or Anathoth:** Towns where the prophets Amos and Jeremiah were born.

"A Dream of Death as an Angel," page 64

> line 18, **then you'll lay your hand upon me:** An ironic reversal of the statement, in the story of the sacrifice of Isaac, when God's angel commands Abraham, "Lay *not* thy hand…" (Genesis 22:12).

"Ecology," page 66

> line 12, *Tashlikh:* The symbolic custom on the last evening of the Jewish New Year of getting rid of last year's sins by emptying crumbs from one's pockets into the sea or river.

*From* "Earth Thoughts in Summer Flow," page 73

> Poem 12, "Naive Painting," line 9, *Av:* Hebrew name of the tenth month in the Jewish calendar. The ninth of Av (*Tisha b'Av*) is a fast day commemorating the destruction of the First and Second Temples in Jerusalem.

"Salt on the Wounds of the Land," page 79

> date: Land Day is an annual day of protest against Israeli confiscation of Arab-owned land. 1976 was the year of the first organized demonstrations in Arab villages.

The poet dressed up as an angel, page 84

> line 3, **the wife of Manoah and the wife of Joseph the carpenter:** The mother of Samson and mother of Jesus.

"Cities on Their Mounds," page 96

> title: Taken from Jeremiah 30:18: *the city shall be rebuilt on its mounds,* that is, on the mound of ruins left after the previous destruction. The modern Hebrew word *tel* ("mound") literally means an archaeological site, a hill built up of many layers of civilization, one layer on top of another. There are many excavations of these sites in Israel.

line 6, **khubeiza:** Arabic name of an herb of the mallow family with edible leaves and fruit.

"Conversation with a Radio," page 103

line 2, *A song I dreamt about Prague:* A Hebrew song written by the popular singer Arik Einstein, after the Soviet invasion of Prague in August 1968 and played on the radio in Israel every August to commemorate the anniversary of that invasion.

"Soliloquy of Dada the Cat," page 105

line 43, **I am what I am:** Rearrangement of the three words in Exodus 3:14, when God first speaks to Moses from the burning bush: *Ehyeh-Asher-Ehyeh* (I am that I am [KJV]).

"Cheese," page 111

lines 32–33: Paraphrase of I Samuel 31:7.

"Burning Holy Books," page 117

title: Written after some hooligans broke into a Tel-Aviv synagogue and set fire to the prayer books. This title was the headline in a religious newspaper.

"River in the Desert," page 121

line 5, *The mane of your hair:* All italicized lines are after Mallarmé's sonnet "Tristesse D'Été."

"The Fowl of the Air," page 122

title: From Genesis 1:26.

"Far from the Flag Parade," page 129

line 4, **Ein-Hatkhelet:** The northernmost suburb of Netanya, where the poet lived as a child. *Avikhail* is the nearest village, separated from that suburb only by its orange groves.

line 7, Shamutti: a variety of orange, big and heavy, with a very thick, rough peel.

*From* "Poems with a Dog," page 130

Poem 1, "Bitch/Armchair," line 12, **a hind let loose:** From Genesis 49:2.

"Jerusalem, 3000," page 137

line 11, **Ehud Olmert:** The Mayor of Jerusalem from 1993 to 2003.

line 13, *capote* and *shtreyml:* Long satin robe and fur hat, typical dress of the Polish nobility in the eighteenth and nineteenth centuries, worn by ultraorthodox Jews.

line 14, **Pale:** The Pale of Settlement, the territory where Jews were confined during the czarist regime in Russia and later in Poland and other parts of eastern Europe.

"The Tel-Aviv Subway," page 138

title: There is no subway in Tel-Aviv. Bureaucracy, budget, and other priorities have prevented it from being built for more than forty years.

"On the Seventy-three," page 142

line 24, *AKA:* The acronym formed from the Hebrew words *Agaf Koakh Adam*—The Manpower Department of the Israel Defense Forces.

| **MEIR WIESELTIER**, the most acclaimed Israeli poet in the generation after Yehuda Amichai, was born in Moscow in 1941 and arrived in the new state of Israel in 1949, growing up in Netanya. At the age of fourteen he moved to Tel-Aviv, where he has lived ever since. His first poems were published when he was eighteen, and he has since published twelve collections of poetry in Hebrew. Although his poems have been translated into many languages and have appeared in English translation in leading American and British journals and anthologies for thirty years, they have not been published in a single volume until now. In addition to his many other honors, he was awarded the Prime Minister's Prize for Literature in 1996, the Bialik Prize in 1995, and the most prestigious achievement award in Israel, the Israel Prize, in 2000. Wieseltier has translated into Hebrew six of Shakespeare's tragedies, which have been performed and published in Israel. He has also translated novels by Charles Dickens, Virginia Woolf, E. M. Forster, and Malcolm Lowry.

| **SHIRLEY KAUFMAN** has published eight volumes of poems in the United States and has won many awards since her first prize-winning collection in 1969, *The Floor Keeps Turning*. Her most recent books are *Roots in the Air: New and Selected Poems*, 1996, and *Threshold*, 2003. She has also published books of translations from the Hebrew of Amir Gilboa and Abba Kovner and collaborated with Judith Herzberg on the translation of Herzberg's Dutch poems, *But What: Selected Poems*, which won a Columbia University Translation prize. She has coedited, and translated with others, *The Defiant Muse: Hebrew Feminist Poems from Antiquity to the Present*, 1999. A former resident of San Francisco, she has lived in Jerusalem since 1973.

| | |
|---:|:---|
| Compositor: | Impressions Book and Journal Services, Inc. |
| Text: | 10.5/15 Adobe Jenson |
| Display: | Eureka Sans |
| Printer and binder: | Thomson-Shore, Inc. |